W9-ATF-068

910
STI

Stienecker, David,
1952-

Countries.

$22.79

34880030000025

DATE			

BAKER & TAYLOR

DISCOVERING GEOGRAPHY

COUNTRIES

DAVID L. STIENECKER

■

ART BY RICHARD MACCABE

BENCHMARK BOOKS

MARSHALL CAVENDISH
NEW YORK

Benchmark Books
Marshall Cavendish Corporation
99 White Plains Road
Tarrytown, New York 10591

©Marshall Cavendish Corporation, 1998

Series created by Blackbirch Graphics, Inc.

Printed and bound in the United States.

Library of Congress Cataloging-in-Publication Data

Stienecker, David.
    Countries / by David L. Stienecker.
        p.   cm. — (Discovering geography)
    Includes index.
    Summary: Introduces the location, resources, animals, and major cities of various countries of the world through facts, maps, riddles, puzzles, and other activities.
    ISBN 0-7614-0542-9 (lib. bdg.)
    1. Geography—Juvenile literature. [1. Geography.]
I. Title. III. Series: Discovering geography (New York, N.Y.)
G133.S834   1998
910'.9—dc21
                                                    97-323
                                                    CIP
                                                    AC

Contents

■ ■ ■ ■ ■ ■ ■

Countries of the World   4

Country Riddles   6

The Capitals of Europe   8

Countries Change   10

Where Are the Animals?   12

Where Does It Come From?   14

Where Do All the People Live?   16

Island Nations   18

Making Country Puzzles   20

What's the Land Like?   22

How High?   24

What's the Climate Like?   26

Animal Maps   28

Answers   29

Glossary   31

Index   32

Countries of the World

There are about 190 countries in the world. The map on page 5 shows several of them. Locate the United States on the map. What country is to the north of the United States? What country is to the south?

Can you answer these questions?

- Hawaii and Alaska are not attached to mainland United States. How can you tell that they are part of the United States?

- Which labeled country is the smallest?

- Which three North American countries share the Gulf of Mexico?

- Which two North American countries have coastlines along the Arctic Ocean?

The colors and lines on the map tell you where the borders of the countries are.

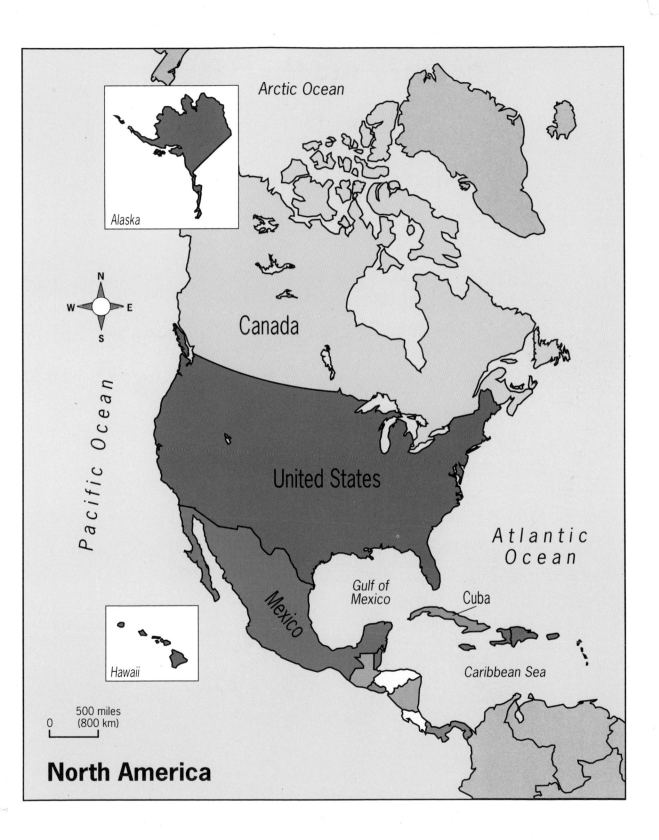

Arctic Ocean

Alaska

N
W   E
S

Canada

Pacific Ocean

United States

Atlantic
Ocean

Gulf of
Mexico

Cuba

Mexico

Hawaii

Caribbean Sea

500 miles
(800 km)
0

North America

Country Riddles

This map shows the countries of Africa.
You can use it to play a riddle game.

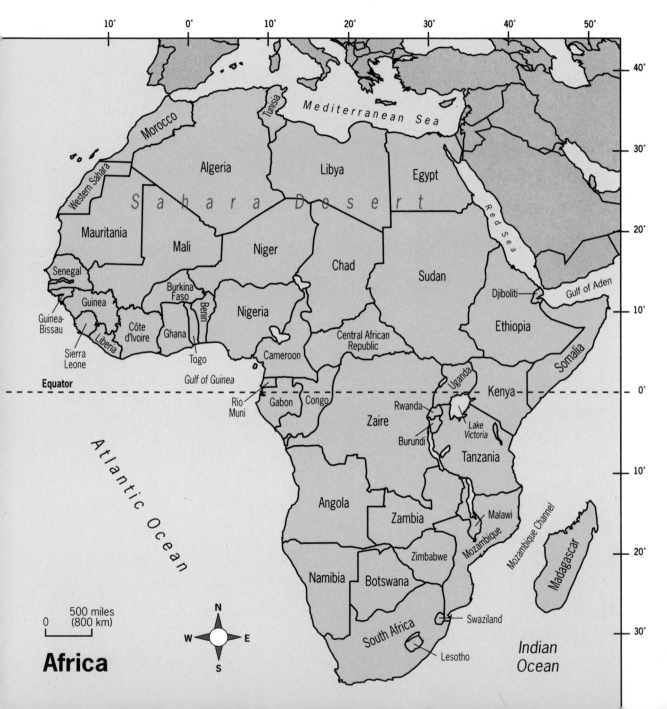

Africa

Each player will need slips of paper and a pencil. Here's how to play:

- Each player selects a country. Don't let the other player know which country it is.

- Each player writes a riddle on a piece of paper about the country he or she has chosen. The riddle could include the names of bordering countries, natural landmarks, lines of latitude and longitude, etc. Use the map to help you decide on your riddle clues. Here are some examples:

  - Part of my country borders on the Indian Ocean. The equator passes right through my middle. What country am I?

  - Part of Lake Victoria is in this country that is bordered by Mozambique. What country am I?

  - 30° N latitude and 30° E longitude cross where I am. What country am I?

- One player reads his or her riddle aloud. The first player to point out the country on the map above wins the round and takes the riddle.

- Play in turn until all the riddles have been solved. The player holding the most riddles at the end of the game wins.

Have each player write two, three, or more riddles and play a longer game.

The equator is 0° latitude— the imaginary line that divides the Northern and Southern hemispheres.

The Capitals of Europe

Each country has a national capital. Look at the map key to find the symbol for a capital city. Then see how many western European countries and capital cities you can find.

- Take a trip through western Europe. Visit the capitals of these European countries. Use your finger to trace a route. Keep a list of the capital cities you visit.

From	To
Spain	France
France	United Kingdom
United Kingdom	Germany
Germany	Italy
Italy	Sweden
Sweden	Finland

- Make your own tour of European capitals. List the countries and their capital cities. Begin and end in the same capital city.

- Make a mega-tour. See how many capital cities you can include on a trip through Europe without ever crossing your route.

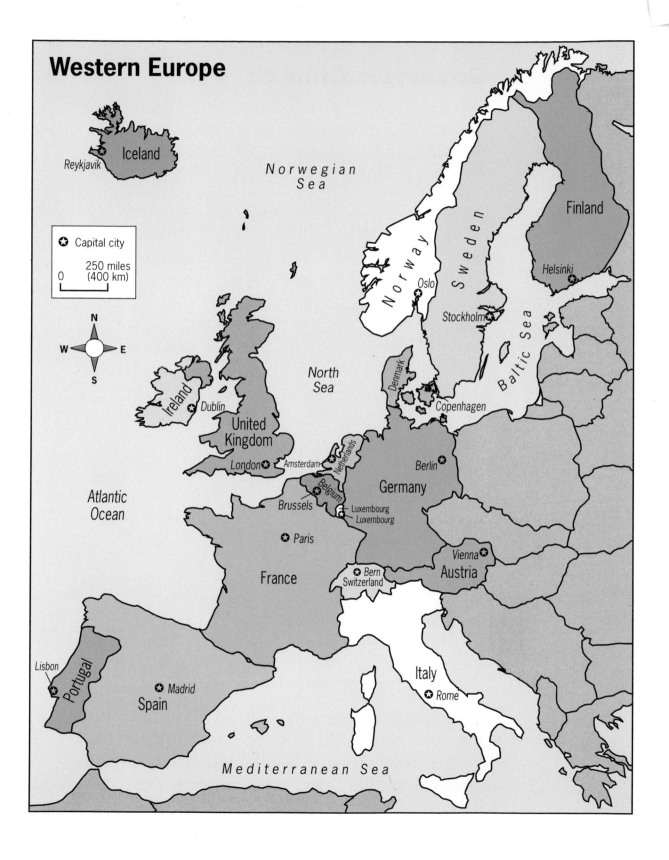

Countries Change

You might think that countries stay pretty much the same. But countries can change. Look at this map of Yugoslavia as it was until 1991.

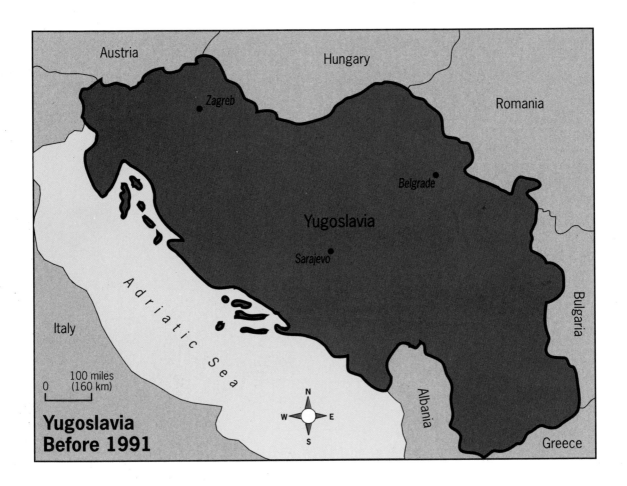

Sometimes new countries form and old countries disappear. Or, a country may change its borders and shape. Usually countries change as the result of a war or some other conflict.

This map shows what Yugoslavia looks like today.

Compare this map with the previous one. See how many countries you can find on this map that are not on the other one.

Yugoslavia Today

- Locate Yugoslavia on the first map. Compare it to the second map. How has Yugoslavia changed?

- What present-day countries used to be part of Yugoslavia?

11

Where Are the Animals?

An endangered animal is one that is threatened with becoming extinct.

There are many endangered animals around the world. The numbers on the map show countries where a few of them can be found.

The pictures below show some endangered animals. Match the numbers next to the pictures with the numbers on the map to locate a country where each animal can be found. Make a chart to show the countries and the endangered animals found in them.

ANIMAL	COUNTRY
BOBCAT	MEXICO
CHEETAH	

1. BOBCAT

2. CHEETAH

3. PANDA

4. PANTHER

5. TIGER

6. INDIGO MACAW

7. CONDOR

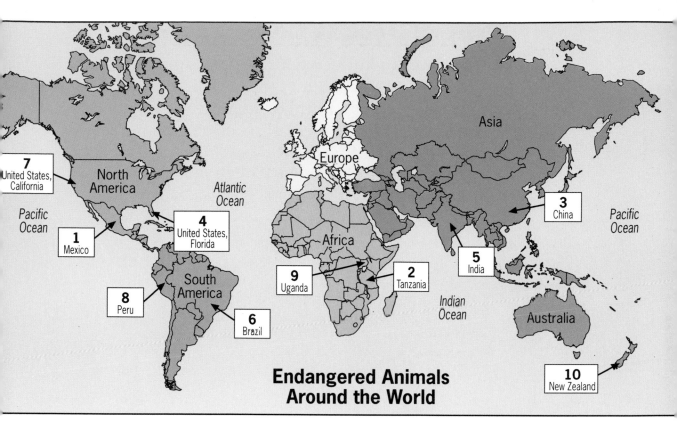

**Endangered Animals
Around the World**

8. VICUÑA

9. GORILLA

10. KAKAPO

Today, at least 120 kinds of mammals and 185 kinds of birds are endangered.

- Select an endangered animal. Do some research and write an article about it.

Where Does It Come From?

If you want to know where things come from, you can look at a product map. This map shows where some familiar natural resources come from. Which natural resources come from the United States?

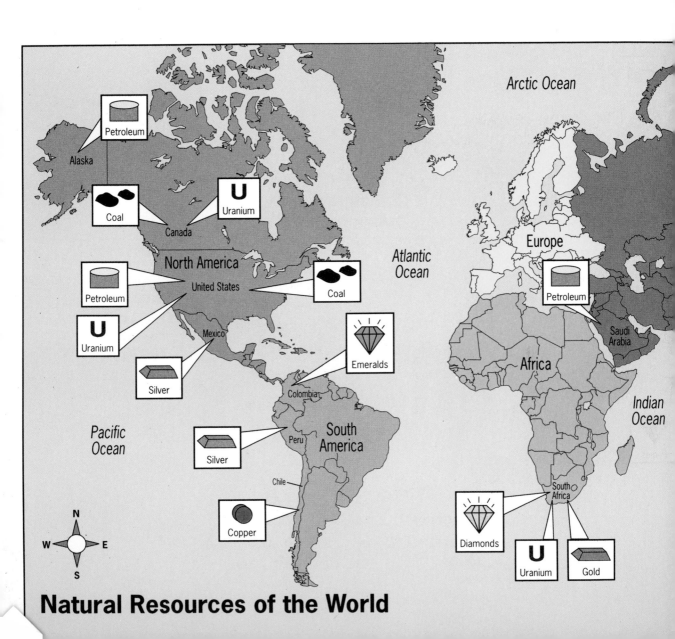

Natural Resources of the World

- Make a chart like this one to show which countries the natural resources shown on the map come from.

Natural Resource	Country
Diamonds	South Africa

A natural resource is a product that people need or use that comes from the Earth.

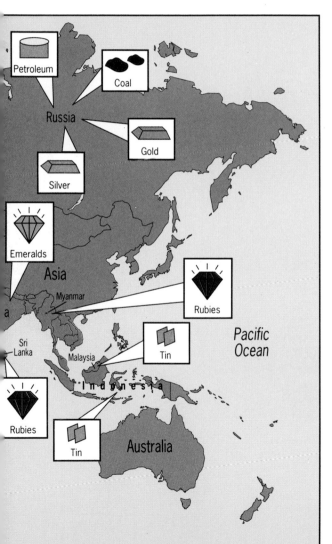

- Make a poster to show what each of the natural resources shown on the map is used for. Do some research if you need to.

- Which natural resources on the map have you come across? What are they used for?

- Pick a country and find out what its natural resources are. Make a map to show where in the country the natural resources come from.

Where Do All the People Live?

If you want to know how the population of the world is distributed, you can look at a population map. This map uses colors to show population densities. Just check the map key to find out what the colors mean.

Persons per square mile:

- Less than 2
- 2 to 25
- 25 to 125
- 125 to 250
- More than 250

500 miles
(800 km)
0

Population of South America

- Locate and name at least three countries where the population density along much of the coastline is 25 to 125 people per square mile.

- Name two parts of South America that have the lowest population density.

- Locate Chile on the map. How many different population densities are there within this country?

- How many people live in the area of South America that surrounds the city of Rio de Janeiro?

- Choose a country. Make a population map. Don't forget to include a map key. Use almanacs or encyclopedias for your information.

Population density is the average number of people who live in each square mile.

About 3/4 of all the people in the world live in Asia and Europe.

In 1996, the world's population was about 5.8 billion.

Island Nations

When most people think of a nation, they don't usually think of it as also being an island. Yet, there are many island nations scattered around the world. The maps on these pages show some nations you've probably heard of.

Great Britain is the eighth-largest island in the world. It is made up of England, Wales, and Scotland. The English Channel separates Great Britain from the rest of Europe. Great Britain along with Northern Ireland make up the United Kingdom.

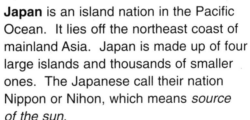

Japan is an island nation in the Pacific Ocean. It lies off the northeast coast of mainland Asia. Japan is made up of four large islands and thousands of smaller ones. The Japanese call their nation Nippon or Nihon, which means *source of the sun*.

Iceland lies just below the Arctic Circle in the North Atlantic Ocean. Iceland is sometimes called the *Land of Frost and Fire* because it has large, icy glaciers as well as steaming hot springs and active volcanoes. Iceland is also called the *Land of the Midnight Sun* because it is light almost 24 hours a day in June, and dark for a similar period in December.

Cuba is an island nation in the West Indies about 90 miles (145 km) south of Florida. It consists of one large island and more than 1,600 smaller ones. Cuba has a beautiful coastline made up of sandy beaches, many bays and inlets, and colorful coral reefs.

New Zealand is an island nation in the Pacific Ocean. Its nearest neighbor is Australia. The Tasman Sea separates the two nations. New Zealand consists of two main islands called the North Island and the South Island. Several dozen smaller islands are also part of New Zealand.

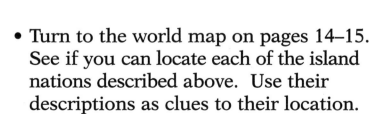

An island is a body of land smaller than a continent and surrounded by water.

- Turn to the world map on pages 14–15. See if you can locate each of the island nations described above. Use their descriptions as clues to their location.

- Choose an island nation that sounds interesting to you. Then do some research and write an article about it. Include a map of the island with your article.

Making Country Puzzles

Make a country puzzle. Carefully trace this map of South America onto a piece of paper. Label each of the countries. Then cut the countries apart to make a puzzle. Mix up the pieces and put the puzzle together.

- Work with one or more friends to put your puzzle together. Take turns picking pieces and deciding where they go.

- Use the puzzle pieces to play a game. Turn the puzzle pieces over and mix them up. Each player in turn takes a puzzle piece and holds it up so the other players can't see the name of the country. The player to name the country first takes the piece. The player with the most pieces at the end of the game wins.

- Make a country puzzle of your own.

Pieces fit together at their borders.

What's the Land Like?

To find out what kind of land a country has, you can look at a terrain map. This terrain map shows the kinds of land for the countries of Africa. How many different kinds of land does the map show? Just check the map key.

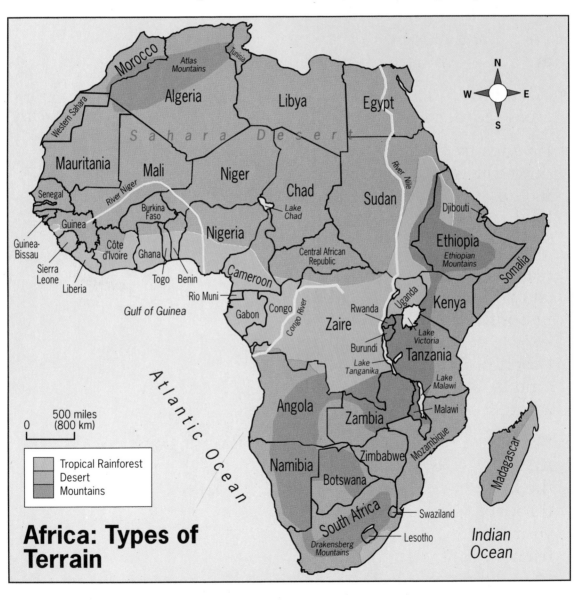

Africa: Types of Terrain

Map key:
- Tropical Rainforest
- Desert
- Mountains

Scale: 500 miles (800 km)

- What things does the map show besides the types of land?

- What color on the map stands for tropical rainforest? How do you know?

- Locate Egypt in the northeast part of Africa. What kind of land do you find there?

- Locate and name three African countries that are almost entirely tropical rainforest.

- What are the names of the mountains that cross Morocco and northern Algeria?

- Imagine that you are taking a sightseeing trip down the River Niger. You begin your journey in Guinea. Name the countries and kind of land you would pass through as you make your way to the coast of Nigeria.

The Sahara is the largest desert in the world.

- Plan an African tour. Your trip should begin in Egypt and end in South Africa. You should visit 12 African countries in all. Describe your route and the kind of land you would travel through in each country.

- Plan a trip of your own through Africa. Name the countries and the kind of land you would travel through. Write directions for your journey. Give them to a friend. See if your friend can trace your route on the map.

How High?

To find out how high a place is, you can look at an elevation map like this one. The different colors on the map show how many feet or meters the land is above or below sea level. The map key unlocks the secret of the colors used on the map. How many elevations does this map show?

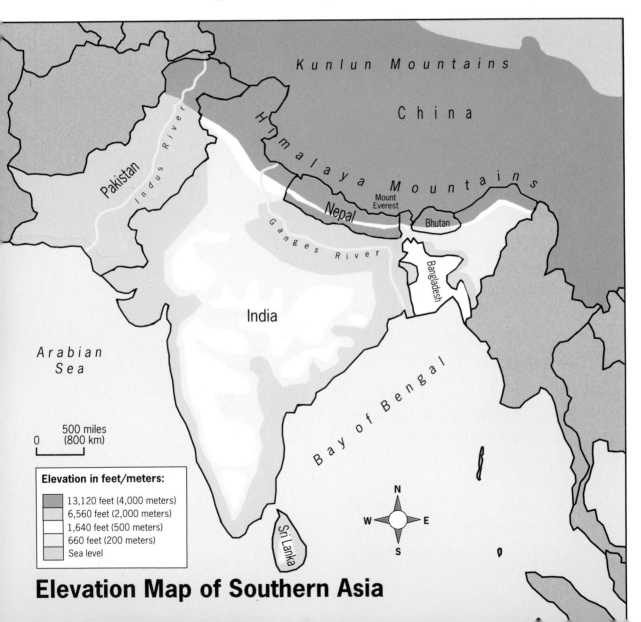

Kunlun Mountains

China

Pakistan

Indus River

Himalaya Mountains

Nepal

Mount Everest

Bhutan

Ganges River

Bangladesh

India

Arabian Sea

Bay of Bengal

500 miles
(800 km)
0

Elevation in feet/meters:

	13,120 feet (4,000 meters)
	6,560 feet (2,000 meters)
	1,640 feet (500 meters)
	660 feet (200 meters)
	Sea level

N

W E

S

Sri Lanka

Elevation Map of Southern Asia

- Which country shown in southern Asia has the highest elevations?

- Locate India on the map. Describe how the elevation changes as you make your way across the country from the Arabian Sea to the Bay of Bengal.

- Locate the Ganges River in northern India. At what elevation does most of this river flow?

- At what level are the coastlines of almost all the countries shown on the map? Why do you think these elevations are similar?

- Play a game. Close your eyes. Then touch the map with your finger. Open your eyes. Identify the country and the elevation where your finger is pointing.

Mt. Everest, on the border of Nepal, is the highest mountain in the world. It rises about 29,029 feet (8,850 meters) above sea level.

What's the Climate Like?

To find out what kind of climate a country has, use a climate map like this one of South America. Like elevation maps, climate maps also use colors to show different climate regions. How many different climate regions are shown for South America? To find out, check the map key.

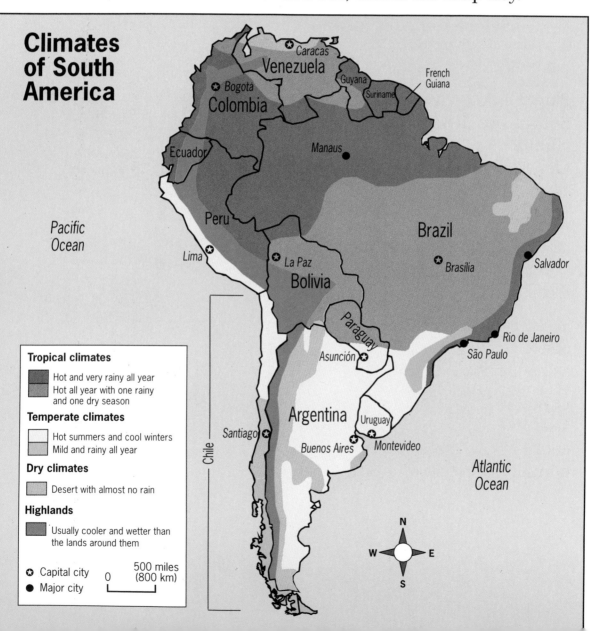

Climates of South America

Pacific Ocean

Atlantic Ocean

Caracas
Venezuela
Bogotá
Colombia
Guyana
Suriname
French Guiana
Ecuador
Manaus
Peru
Brazil
Lima
La Paz
Brasília
Salvador
Bolivia
Paraguay
Rio de Janeiro
São Paulo
Asunción
Argentina
Uruguay
Santiago
Buenos Aires
Montevideo
Chile

Tropical climates
- Hot and very rainy all year
- Hot all year with one rainy and one dry season

Temperate climates
- Hot summers and cool winters
- Mild and rainy all year

Dry climates
- Desert with almost no rain

Highlands
- Usually cooler and wetter than the lands around them

⊗ Capital city
● Major city

500 miles
0   (800 km)

N
W ← → E
S

- Brazil has five climate regions. See if you can identify them on the map. Make a list.

- In what kind of climate region are the capital cities of these countries located: Venezuela, Brazil, Paraguay, Argentina, and Chile.

- Which country has the largest area of tropical climate? Which country has the largest area of dry climate?

- Play a game with a friend. Select a South American country. Describe its climate regions. See if your friend can identify the country.

- If you were going to live anywhere in South America, which climate region would you choose? Which country or countries would have the climate you liked best?

- Select one South American country. Make a climate map using the map above as reference. Make up your own map key.

- Make a climate map of South America. Use colored construction paper to show each climate region. Display your climate map like a poster.

Climate is the weather over a long period of time.

Parts of Argentina have the hottest weather in South America.

Animal Maps

Maps can show where certain plants and animals live in a country. This map shows where some of Australia's animals live.

- Name three animals that live along Australia's eastern coast.

- If you were searching for an echidna, in what part of Australia might you look?

- Budgerigar, which we call parakeets, live in large flocks in Australia. In which part of Australia would you find them?

- What is your favorite animal on the map? In which part of Australia would you go to see it?

Answers

Pps. 4–5, Countries of the World
Canada is to the north of the United States. Mexico is to the south.
By the color pink.
Cuba.
United States, Mexico, and Cuba.
United States (Alaska) and Canada.

Pps. 6–7, Country Riddles
Kenya; Tanzania; Egypt.

Pps. 8–9, The Capitals of Europe
Answers will vary.

Pps. 10–11, Countries Change
Yugoslavia has become smaller. Macedonia, Bosnia-Herzegovina, Croatia, and Slovenia used to be part of Yugoslavia.

Pps. 12–13, Where Are the Animals?
1. bobcat—Mexico; 2. cheetah—Tanzania; 3. panda—China;
4. Florida panther—U.S.; 5. tiger—India; 6. indigo macaw—Brazil;
7. California condor—U.S.;
8. vicuna—Peru; 9. mountain gorilla—Uganda; 10. kakapo—New Zealand

Pps.14–15, Where Does It Come From?
Petroleum, coal, and uranium come from the United States.

Natural Resource	Country
Diamonds	South Africa
Gold	South Africa, Russia
Silver	Mexico, Peru, Russia
Emeralds	Colombia, India
Rubies	Myanmar, Sri Lanka
Petroleum	Russia, United States, Saudi Arabia
Coal	Russia, United States, Canada
Tin	Malaysia, Indonesia
Copper	Chile
Uranium	United States, Canada, South Africa

Pps. 16–17, Where Do All the People Live?
Venezuela, Colombia, Ecuador, Peru, and Brazil.

The lowest population densities are in the central northwest, and the southern tip.

There are three different population densities in Chile.

More than 250 people per square mile.

Pps. 18–19, Island Nations

No answers.

Pps. 20–21, Making Country Puzzles

No answers.

Pps. 22–23, What's the Land Like?

The map shows rivers and lakes and the names of mountains and deserts. It also shows the names of African countries and their borders.

The map key shows that tropical rainforests are shown with dark green.

Egypt is mostly desert.

Sierra Leone, Liberia, Ghana, Togo, Benin, Cameroon, Rio Muni, Gabon, Congo, Zaire, and Uganda are almost all tropical rainforest.

The Atlas Mountains cross Morocco and northern Algeria.

Start in Guinea, pass into desert in Mali and Niger, and pass from desert to tropical rainforest in Nigeria.

Pps. 24–25, How High?

The map shows five elevations.

China has the highest elevations in Asia.

Begin at sea level. Pass into elevations of 660 feet (200 meters), 1,640 feet (500 meters), 660 feet (200 meters), and back to sea level.

The Ganges River flows through land at sea level.

The coastlines of almost all the countries on the map are at sea level.

This is because the coastal areas drop down to the same level as the sea.

Pps. 26–27, What's the Climate Like?

This map shows six climate regions for South America.

The climate regions of Brazil are: Hot all year with one rainy season and one dry season; hot and very rainy all year; desert with almost no rain; hot summers and cool winters; mild and rainy all year.

Caracas, Venezuela—desert with almost no rain
Brasilia, Brazil—hot all year with one rainy season and one dry season
Asuncion, Paraguay—hot summers and cool winters
Buenos Aires, Argentina—hot summers and cool winters
Santiago, Chile—desert with almost no rain

Brazil has the largest area of tropical climate. Argentina has the largest area of dry climate.

P. 28, Animal Maps

Cuscus, kookaburra, koala, and brolga crane live along Australia's east coast.

You would look in the southwest for echidnas.

Budgerigars live on the south central coast of Australia.

Glossary

border The boundary of a state or country.

climate The weather of a place over a long period of time.

continent One of seven great land masses on the Earth.

country All the land of a nation united under the same government.

elevation How high a place is above the Earth's surface.

endangered animal An animal that is threatened with extinction.

equator The imaginary line that divides the Northern and Southern hemispheres; 0° latitude.

island A body of land smaller than a continent that is surrounded by water.

map key A list that explains the meaning of the symbols used on a map.

natural resource A product that people need or use that comes from the Earth.

population density The average number of people who live in a given area.

sea level The level of the surface of the sea. Places on Earth are measured as so many feet or meters above or below sea level.

terrain The physical or geographical features of an area of land.

Index

A
animal maps, 28

B
borders, 4, 10, 25

C
capitals, 8
climate, 26, 27
climate map, 26, 27
climate regions, 26, 27
coastlines, 4, 17, 19, 25
continent, 19

E
elevation map, 24, 26
elevations, 24, 25
endangered animals, 12–13
equator, 7

I
island, 18, 19
island nations, 18–19

L
lines of latitude, 7
lines of longitude, 7

M
map key, 8, 16, 17, 22, 24, 26,
    27

N
natural resources, 14–15

P
population density, 16, 17
population map, 16, 17
product maps, 14

S
sea level, 24, 25

T
terrain map, 22